Visions of India

William Simpson in
Indian dress, 1874.

Visions of India

THE SKETCHBOOKS OF WILLIAM SIMPSON 1859-62

MILDRED ARCHER

Introduction by

PAUL THEROUX

Salem House Publishers
Topsfield, Massachusetts

First published in the United States by Salem House Publishers, 1986,
462 Boston Street, Topsfield, MA 01983.

Library of Congress Catalog Card Number:
86-61018
ISBN: 0 88162 205 2

This book was designed and produced by
John Calmann and King Ltd, London

Typeset by Tek Art, England
Printed in Singapore by Imago Productions (FE) Co Pte

CONTENTS

PREFACE

The reproductions in this book are taken mainly from William Simpson's small sketchbooks, all of which are dated. Three of these record his journey up country from Calcutta, his first and second Himalayan tours, his journey down country and his tours of Central India and Bombay. Sadly, the fourth sketchbook, covering South and Western India, cannot be traced. The gap can, however, be filled by drawings from a bound volume in the Prints and Drawings Department of the Victoria and Albert Museum containing 387 larger sketches which Simpson himself assembled after his return to England, as well as the photograph and lively title page reproduced here. The sketches are further supplemented by a number of finished watercolours in the Indian Department of the Victoria and Albert Museum, the India Office Library and numerous private collections. In two cases the original sketch and the worked-up watercolour derived from it are reproduced for comparison on facing pages. Complete sets of the chromo-lithographs whose production Simpson supervised are held in both the Victoria and Albert Museum and the India Office Library; one is reproduced in this book.

I would like to express my gratitude to John Goelet for permission to reproduce the drawings from the sketchbooks in his possession. I must also thank Niall Hobhouse for the original suggestion for this book and for his most generous help and advice. The Victoria and Albert Museum and the India Office Library were extremely helpful and I thank these institutions and their staff, especially Betty Tyers, who alerted me to the watercolours in her care. Above all, I am grateful to Peter Zombory-Moldovan for his sensitive editing of the text.

Mildred Archer
March 1986

The quotations in the text are taken from William Simpson's *Autobiography* (see Bibliography). Where appropriate, the spelling of Indian place-names has been modernised to accord with current usage. All reproductions, unless indicated otherwise, are of works in pencil and watercolour. Where two dates are given in the captions, the first (in brackets) indicates the probable date of Simpson's visit.

Introduction

❧

BY PAUL THEROUX

WILLIAM SIMPSON was born and raised in a Glasgow slum, but he was one of those indestructible Scots whose lives were shaped for the better by their disadvantages. The man never stopped working, and he was brilliant at what he did. Unlike most self-made men he had a sense of humour; and he was modest – not a ranter, not abrasive. He seems to have been very tolerant and easy-going, rare qualities in someone who was obviously a workaholic. He started with nothing – he had no standing, no influence, and he got little help. His education lasted just over one year. This condition gave him a peculiar hunger and curiosity. The Victorian age produced many remarkable artist-travellers, and Simpson was one of the best of them – truthful, intrepid, and very talented. He took nothing for granted.

If he had a fault it was his intense sense of privacy, but this is not unusual in someone who seemed virtually to have come from nowhere. Such people often develop a habit of secrecy, for why should anyone want to know of the dullness, the sadness, the humiliation of having nothing? This reticence of Simpson's is unhelpful for anyone writing about him, because there is so much in the foreground and so little in the background – and come to think of it, his pictures are a bit that way, too.

But, of course, starting nowhere with nothing is impossible. Although he says little about his family, the details he lets drop must convince us that they were loyal and kind, that his father inspired him, and his grandmother taught him. In a very likeable appendix to his autobiography he describes life in a Glasgow *land* or tenement in the 1820s – his friends, his fun, the children's songs and games. One can see that he had close friends and that people were kind to him, and that all this helped give him a good beginning.

But the fact that he gave instructions for his autobiography to be published only after his death is evidence of his judiciousness, and it can only have been an unnecessary delay: the book covers the high spots of his career – nothing personal, and no revelations. Yet this in itself is revealing, for who is more welcome as a friend and fellow traveller than a person of tact and discretion? He did not mutter, he did not whisper, he did not dine out on his stories about the grand and the glorious – and he could easily have done so, because he travelled in the close company of aristocrats and royalty, and most palaces were open to him. Nothing is more revealing of character than the experience of travel. For example, just after the Crimean War, he travelled through Circassia with the Duke of Newcastle; but, typically, he tells us only about Circassia and the Circassians. No gossip, nothing trivial, no broken confidences, no froth: that decency he had brought from the Glasgow tenement.

Still, a little detail would have been welcome. We know from the chance remark of an editor that Simpson married late in life; but we don't know when or where that was, we know nothing of the courtship, and we don't know the woman's name. The marriage is not even mentioned in Simpson's entry in the *Dictionary of National Biography*. There is a single allusion to the wife in Simpson's autobiography, but that book is dedicated to his only child, his daughter, Anne Penelope. There is a tenderness in the dedication that suggests that he was devoted to the child. He arrived in London when he was in his late twenties, but travel took up so much of his time that he did not actually buy a house and settle down until he was in his sixties. This was in Willesden – no trace of him there.

His books are out of print, his pictures hardly known. Poor Simpson! And yet one suspects that Simpson would be very philosophical about this, for, though he had plenty of self-respect, he was a man who had no vanity at all.

❧

Simpson was the first war-artist. In a sense we know more of the Crimean War from Simpson's lithographs than from Alexander Kinglake's many volumes of official history. But Simpson was also a prolific writer, a journalist, amateur archeologist, and a watercolourist of distinction. Above all, he was an eye-witness in an age of great events. His career spanned the triumphant and turbulent years of Victoria's reign, from the war in which he earned the name 'Crimean' Simpson, to the Queen's Jubilee, just a few years before he died. He went everywhere, he saw everything, he met everyone; and he was not a snob, so 'everyone' meant just that – dervishes, kings, princesses, pioneers, camel drivers, mad Irishmen, predatory Kurds, the Shah of Persia and the King of Abyssinia. He was particularly skilful at talking to – and sketching – rebels and outlaws. He had courage, a strong stomach and a nose for what the public wanted. When he was touring San

Francisco in 1873 he got wind of the war between the Modoc Indians and American troops – this was near the Oregon state-line. One of the pictures he supplied to his employer, the *Illustrated London News*, was of an odd, tangled and uprooted-looking thing like an oversize divot whacked out of the ground by a very strong, very bad golfer. The description reads, 'Scalp of Scaur-faced Charlie, Modoc Chief . . .'

He was also very interested in religion. He wrote a book about symbolism in the story of Jonah and the whale – and other stories in which men are swallowed by sea-creatures. He wrote a learned monograph about the Buddhist praying wheel, and about wheel symbolism in general. While covering the first Afghan War and sending back sketches of battles and marches, he also managed to carry out pioneering excavations. He was fascinated by mounds, and tombs, and caves. He went to Jerusalem to look at digs, and unearthed part of ancient India, and reported on Schliemann's Troy – indeed, he was practically alone in disputing Schliemann's claim that the mud dwelling in Mycenae could be King Priam's palace. He was one of the first to suggest what many people said later – and he was right – about Schliemann being impatient and rather bogus.

Simpson's father was a poor working-man, but it was a stroke of luck that he worked in a printing shop, because it meant that his son would do something similar, and that led the boy into lithography. Young William had a glimpse of better things, and wanted them. He was apprenticed to a lithographer and that highly specialised skill inspired his drawing and painting. From the age of 15 or so he was saving his dinner penny, and instead of buying baps he bought tubes of water-colour paint. He sketched from nature and later drew pictures of the old houses of Glasgow – that was the beginning of his lifelong interest in history and archaeology. After the houses were pulled down, only Simpson's pictures remained as a record of old Glasgow, in Stuart's *Views of Glasgow* (1848). He read poetry and literary criticism, attended night classes somewhat fitfully, and became a devotee of Ruskin. He spent his days working as a lithographer and his time off hiking and sketching. In *Meeting the Sun* (1874), he wrote,

My first love in art was a Highland mountain, and I have been a mountain worshipper ever since. Fate has privileged me to visit many shrines of this faith, – the Alps, the Caucasus, the Himalayas, the mountains of Abyssinia; now I can add to this list Fuji-yama in Japan, and the Sierra Nevadas of California, where I have seen Mount Shasta and the Yosemite Valley. I think that a valley, however beautiful it may be, never could have become a sacred object, such as mountains seem to have been all over the world. A great high peak, soaring up into Heaven, with its garments of snow, white and pure, often lost in the clouds, as if communing with those above, its icy barriers setting it apart like consecrated ground where the profane must not tread, – these are the features of the higher mountains, which may have impressed men and produced that religious veneration of which we have evidences from the most remote antiquity.

He sold his first watercolour, 'The Braes of Lochaber', in 1850.

Naturally ambitious and seeking a challenge, he set off for London in 1851, and in the metropolis found work in a large firm of lithographers. He was at pains to point out in his autobiography the importance of lithography. It was exclusively pictorial, concerned with people and events ('Now it is all done by photography,' he said in 1893). Of lithography he wrote, 'The startling thing is that it was a class of work which came into existence, lasted only a quarter of a century, and has entirely vanished.' And he remarked on how lithographers frequently became artists, while engravers seldom did.

The Crimean War gave him his first great break. In London he had been sketching pictures of battles for readers, basing them on newspaper accounts. He read the papers, mugged up the topography and tried to depict the action. He kept wishing he were there at the front. He said to his employers, 'Here they are making "gabions", "fascines", "traverses", etcetera. What are these? No one knows. If I were there I could send sketches of them, so that everyone would understand.'

He was sent, and two days before his thirty-first birthday he was under fire at Balaclava. He was very brave; he sketched while being shelled. But he was not foolish – just very rational and downright. 'If a shell is coming to you,' he said, 'it becomes instantly visible, as a black speck against the white smoke of the gun which fired it, and before it reaches you there is plenty of time to go under cover.'

He earned the respect of Lord Raglan, who allowed Simpson to use the official letter-bag for sending his pictures back to London. And he learned the paradoxes of war. He discovered that it was essential that he see battles for himself because often two officers in a skirmish would disagree on the details and conduct of the action. And at the battle of Tchernaya he noted that in spite of heavy shelling and numerous casualties there was no blood visible on the battleground. The uniforms and dust absorbed it. During the war he was able to spend three weeks at Kertch, visiting and sketching mound tombs – one of his passions. He did not see Miss Nightingale, he said ('she was at Scutari'), but he did see the elderly mulatto Mrs Seacole, and an odd Irishman, one of the casualties of the Crimea. It is characteristic of Simpson's interest in the unusual and out-of-the-way that he gives a vague description of the British commanders yet offers a vivid portrait of this madman:

> He had wrought himself into a state of madness. In the village he had picked up a long stick – a wooden hay-fork formed by the natural branch of the tree. With this clenched in both hands, and his eyes staring wildly out of his head, he was rushing about, exclaiming, 'I smashes whatever I sees'; and whatever could be smashed with the hay-fork was destroyed by this maniac. Glass windows were special attractions to him. I saw him chase a very small fowl, and each time he failed to catch it he became more excited. At last the miserable chicken, exhausted with the chase, fell into his hands, and when this took place the wild fool did not know what to do with it. In an incoherent way he expressed himself as wishing to know what could be done, and at last, grasping the bird by the neck and squeezing it with all his strength, he said, 'Die! Die! Die!'

Another memorable portrait (and of course Simpson sketched these people as well as writing about them) was that of the Kurd he met near Batoum (now the Soviet city of Batumi) on the Black Sea. This Kurd had a face that was 'vile, wicked and cruel', and when asked what he was doing there he said simply, 'killing people'.

> 'Who do you kill?'
> 'Travellers.'
> 'How do you kill them?'
> 'I watch the road, and when I see travellers coming I hide behind a rock and shoot them as they pass.'
> 'How many have you killed?'
> 'Thirteen, and five Russians.'
> He did not explain the reason why he made a distinction in the case of the Russians. It may have been perhaps some patriotic sentiment. He was then asked what he was doing in Batoum.
> To which he replied, 'Some business.'
> 'Where are you going when you leave this place?'
> 'Back to the mountains, where, please God, I hope to shoot some more travellers.'

Simpson had amassed an enormous number of pictures, including rarities, for he had recorded the fall of Sebastopol and had travelled in unknown Circassia. He was able to publish a pictorial history of the war (two folio volumes, 80 plates) and his reputation as a war-artist was made. He was something of a novelty, too, though in a different respect. He had grown a beard, and boys in the street bleated like goats or else called out, 'Doormats!' because 'anyone with a beard was looked upon as Jew or a foreigner'.

After the Crimea, whenever there was a great event to be depicted in a lithograph for the London weekly papers, Simpson was sent. He did everything that came his way: the opening of a canal, a tunnel, or a bridge; wars and uprisings; weddings, coronations, funerals, state visits, or following a royal progress. Simpson faithfully recorded these events, but he did much else besides – sketching ruins and back streets or simply picturesque views. In Japan, later in his life, he tramped around doing views of Fuji.

When Simpson was sent to India to record the aftermath of the Mutiny he had in mind a large-scale project, so that he might do for India what his fellow-countryman David Roberts had done for the Holy Land. He had a grand scheme and envisioned four large volumes with something like 250 plates.

He was at it seven years – three years in India and four years working his sketches into finished pieces. He travelled all over India – to Lahore and Peshawar and up the Khyber Pass; to Simla and, sixteen marches beyond it, to the Sutlej. He sketched Thugs in Jabalpur and then set off in a dooley (a sort of light palanquin) for the wild in-between places ('It is in these spaces that the real India exists'). He travelled to Bhilsa, to find Buddhist architecture, and to the source of the Ganges in the Himalayas, and to out-of-the-way Chitor, before the railway. All the while, he was sketching. He estimated that on his Indian journey he covered 22,570 miles.

The project was, in financial terms, an almost total disaster, and I think that its failure is one of the reasons why Simpson is so obscure a figure today. It was Simpson's awful fate that his Indian pictures remained largely unpublished. His putative publisher, Day's, had gone bust, but the firm regarded Simpson's pictures as their property, and they were simply sold off as bankrupt stock. In spite of this reverse, Simpson kept on. If the Crimea had made him a war-artist, the India trip of 1859-62 made him an artist-traveller in the tradition of the Daniells, Chinnery, Lear, Zoffany, William Purser, Henry Salt, and so many others who made their name bringing pictures of India and the Far East back to England. Some of these were greater artists than Simpson, but no traveller had more stamina, and none was so fastidiously truthful. Simpson's counterpart today is the inspired photographer who travels widely and reports on places that are little-known and dangerous.

Travel also vindicated Simpson's fair-mindedness. He believed he held 'exceptional' views on the subject of national character: in a word, he was not a racist, and he felt very strongly that it was politicians who whipped up feelings of nationalism and xenophobia. He said that as a child he had always been told of the 'superiority of the Scotch'. But it was all prejudice and political humbug. He was not taken in: 'I saw that each country remembered only its own virtues, and saw mainly the vices of its neighbours and, by contrasting the good features of its own character with the bad of the others, reached what was to it a satisfactory conclusion.' His humanity made him clear-sighted, and this shows in his pictures. He travelled around the world without preconceived notions of who or what he would find; and this absence of cant and bigotry in his nature made him a brilliant observer.

> I long ago came to the conclusion that there is more resemblance than difference among the various peoples of the world, and here is what I take to be a characteristic example. In passing through the palace [of the Maharajah Runbir Singh] . . . I had to cross an open court. On the first day I saw a boy mending a defect in the pavement with chunam or kunkur of some kind. The hole was only about six inches or a foot in size, and the boy sat there pounding the chunam slowly into it. I think I spoke to him in passing. Next day I again found him slowly beating away at the same hole. I said something about such a small hole not being yet finished, and his reply was, 'Ha Sahib, Sircar ke-kam hai' – 'It is Government work, sir.' It struck me on hearing those words that it was not the first time I had met that boy.

He made two more visits to India, but by this time he was 'special artist' on a retainer from the *Illustrated London News*. This picture magazine was for most people a window on the world, and under its auspices Simpson went as far afield as Afghanistan (he covered the First Afghan War and, later, the Afghan Boundary Commission) and China; and in 1873 he went completely around the world, the journey he recorded in *Meeting the Sun*, a delightful travel book full of excitements and adventures, off the beaten track (up the Yangtse River, among the Modoc Indians in northern California) and on it (Niagara Falls and the marriage of the Emperor of China).

Simpson was happier among outlaws than he was among royalty. As a guest of the Prince of Wales in a royal residence he worried that the servant assigned to him (because he had none) would take a dim view of his darned socks and his plain old hair brushes – and he cringed at the thought of 'a gorgeous creature in blue plush breeches' unpacking his portmanteau. He preferred the dervish in the caravanserai or the floor-mender in Kashmir. This is the reason his pictures are full of interesting detail, and it also accounts for the fact that Simpson – not a natural writer – produced good travel books. Simply, he talked to everyone and reported faithfully what they said.

That Modoc business turned him into a listener. It was a bitter war and it was particularly bloody for its being so far from any large settlement. But Simpson was not put off by the remoteness of this bloodbath. When the railway ran out, Simpson took a stage-coach, stopping at settlers' log-houses on the way. He met all the usual settler belligerence, but, typically, reported it with irony. In one place, an old settler

> expressed the usual warm desire to see the Modocs exterminated, and included the whole race of Indians in the same merciful sentiment. When he came to the place first there were lots of Indians about – they were as plentiful as ground-squirrels, and every fall white men used to go out and shoot a hundred or two of them. At the present moment he was sorry he could not get away . . . I reported this valiant warrior's wish at the camp, and there was a great regret that such valuable services were not to be had.

That twinkle, that tone of voice and light touch – even some of the expressions – are very Kiplingesque. Though their paths did not cross, Kipling and Simpson travelled many of the same routes in the world, and their enthusiasms, their pawky humour, and the colours they favoured are very similar. Kipling and Simpson shared an interest in Biblical history and classical scholarship, and they were both machine-mad, too – loving the mechanisms of locomotives and tunnelling equipment. Although Simpson was born almost forty years before Kipling, their experience of India overlapped, and their sympathies were much the same – not the pink, princely India, but India outdoors, in its streets and hills and bazaars. Kipling's father illustrated some of his son's work, but how much more appropriate Simpson's pictures would have been. I intend it as praise, but I also mean to suggest his limitations and his quirks, when I say that I regard William Simpson as the Kipling of watercolourists.

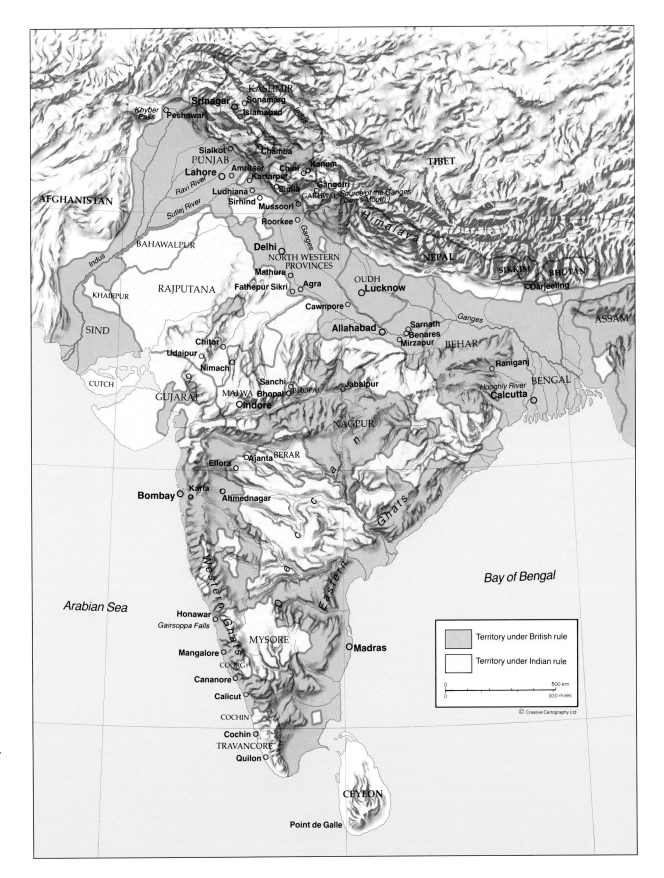

Map of India in 1857.

KASHMIR
Srinagar○ Sonamarg
  ○ Islamabad

Khyber
Pass Peshawar○

TIBET

Sialkot○ Chamba○
PUNJAB
Lahore○ Amritsar○ Chini○ Kanum○
  ○ Kartarpur
Ravi River Simla○ Gangotri○
AFGHANISTAN Ludhiana○ GARHWAL Source of the Ganges (Cow's Mouth)
Sutlej River Sirhind○ Mussoori○ Himalaya
  Roorkee○
  NEPAL
BAHAWALPUR Delhi○ SIKKIM BHUTAN
  NORTH WESTERN
  PROVINCES ○Darjeeling
Indus Mathura○
KHAIRPUR RAJPUTANA Fathepur Sikri ○Agra OUDH
  Lucknow○ ASSAM
SIND Cawnpore○ Ganges
  Sarnath
  Allahabad○ Benares○ Raniganj○
  Chitor○ Mirzapur○ BEHAR
CUTCH Udaipur○ Hooghly River BENGAL
  Nimach○ Sanchi Jabalpur○ Calcutta●
GUJARAT MALWA Bhopal○ ○BHOPAL
  Indore○ NAGPUR

  Ellora○ Ajanta○ BERAR
  Karla○
Bombay○ Ahmednagar○
  Eastern Ghats
Arabian Sea Western Ghats Bay of Bengal

Honawar○
Gairsoppa Falls MYSORE
Mangalore○ Madras●
  COORG
Cananore○
Calicut○
  COCHIN Territory under British rule
Cochin○ Territory under Indian rule
TRAVANCORE
Quilon○ 0   500 km
  0   300 miles
  © Creative Cartography Ltd

  CEYLON

Point de Galle

9

'A large and important work'

———————————•)———————————

The Indian Mutiny of 1857 was followed by the abolition of the East India Company and the passing of the India Act of 1858, by which the government of India passed to the British Crown. As William Simpson himself wrote, 'the public was interested in the cause of the Mutiny, and in everything connected with the people of India. More interest had been excited in England about that country than had ever existed before.'

The firm of P. and D. Colnaghi had recently had a great success with Simpson's book on the Crimea. No doubt mindful of the £12,000 profit which, Simpson learned, Colnaghi had made, discussions took place early in 1859 between Simpson and William Day, whose firm had printed the Colnaghi book. They decided that, in view of the momentous events in India, the time was ripe for 'a large and important work that should do justice to such a subject'. Simpson had, in any case, been itching to travel to the East ever since his return from Circassia four years earlier, and he was delighted with the new commission. The book was to consist of four folio volumes containing some 250 illustrations, along the lines of Daniel Roberts' successful work on the Holy Land and Egypt; even this was to be surpassed, however, for the recent development of chromolithography meant that 'the new work should be in colour, and that the pictures should be more or less reproductions of the originals'. The price was to be an astronomical forty guineas. The prestige and prospects of the venture received an invaluable boost when Queen Victoria, who had taken a lively interest in Simpson's work in the Crimea, to the extent of personally discussing a commission with him, took the unusual step of allowing the book to be dedicated to her in advance of publication. Simpson paid numerous visits to the East India Company's splendid library at India House in Leadenhall Street, where he studied the work of previous artists who had gone to India and produced lavish books of views, most notably the great *Oriental Scenery* of 1795-7 by Thomas and William Daniell. He was by now planning a journey of at least two years; and his researches convinced him that he should undertake not merely a report on the sites and aftermath of the Mutiny, but a far more ambitious survey in pictures of the subcontinent – its landscapes, monuments, its people and their way of life – and to preserve a record of the 'old' India that he sensed was to be irrevocably transformed by the impact of British imperial rule.

Letters of instruction to Lord Canning, the Governor-General, and to Lord Clyde, Commander-in-Chief, were obtained, and Simpson set sail on the *Newcastle*, bound for Calcutta via the Cape.

Frontispiece by William Simpson to an album of his sketches.

Up Country

OCTOBER 1859 TO MARCH 1860

Simpson arrived in Calcutta on 29 October 1859. The *Newcastle* continued to be useful for it was by climbing to the maintop that he managed to obtain a general view of the city (Fig. 1). He drew Government House (Fig. 2), made an excursion out of the city to a nearby village and visited a school which had recently been opened (Fig. 3). He went to Barrackpore House, the Governor-General's country house up the Hooghly river, and sketched its garden (Fig. 4). This was of topical interest as it was there that, during the most worrying days of the Mutiny, Lady Canning had stayed while her husband was up-country, endeavouring to distract her troubled mind from events by tending her garden and making flower-studies. Simpson's sketch shows the garden with its little neo-classical Temple of Fame built by Lord Minto.

The Governor-General and his wife had already left Calcutta on the start of a long tour to meet the Princes who had remained loyal to the British during the Mutiny. Simpson set off up-country to meet him. The first 120 miles, as far as Raniganj, were on the recently begun railway; but from there on, travel was by road – 'and a very fine road it is', Simpson commented approvingly, though he noted that it was about to be rendered obsolete by the railway: 'In our days transitions come quickly, even in India.'

The Delhi he reached on 29 November was a city 'depopulated by the siege'. His first task was to record the sites that had become household names in Britain during the uprising. There was the Kashmir Gate on the north side of the Fort (Fig. 5), which had been the scene of desperate fighting during the assault on the city by the forces under John Nicholson hardly a year before. The Lahore Gate at the end of the Chandni Chauk on the west side of the Fort (Fig. 8) had also seen heavy fighting. The red sandstone Mausoleum of the Emperor Humayun (Fig. 12) was also well known to the British public, for it was here that Major Hodson, after the capture of the city, had received the surrender of Bahadur Shah, the last of the Mughal emperors. Other sketches (Figs. 6, 7) depict the shattered remnants of the buildings that had been used as strongpoints by the British during the fighting. Simpson's lodgings, with Major Walter Fane, himself an enthusiastic amateur artist, were near the Lal Kuan (Fig. 11), in a house that had remained 'unclaimed' since its owner was killed during the siege. Simpson wandered round the city, sketching various well-known streets including Burra Daribah (Fig. 9) and Chandni Chauk (Fig. 10).

As Lord and Lady Canning had by now set off for Lahore to honour the Chiefs of the Punjab who had kept the British supply lines from Delhi open throughout the conflict, Simpson left the city on 14 January to follow. He stopped on the way to draw the canal at Roorkee, (Fig. 13) which had recently been completed. By the evening of the next day he had arrived at the Governor-General's camp at Shaikabad. Here a splendid durbar was held when the Cis-Sutlej chiefs of Patiala (Fig. 14), Jhind (Fig. 15) and Nabha were received by Lord Canning. As Simpson noted, 'the rajahs wore their most gorgeous array – kincob or cloth of gold, and jewels in profusion, and each was attended by a numerous sawari of mounted attendants, elephants, etc.,' a dazzling subject for a painting. From here the party moved on to Sirhind, which had been a flourishing city in Mughal times and had many fine buildings, among them the temple (Fig. 16) that Simpson sketched. As a result of Lady Canning's interest in painting, Simpson was delighted to find that sketching was regarded as a serious daily event and 'it appeared at times as if the whole camp was merely a gigantic sketching excursion'. In the evening all the sketches were produced for criticism by the assembled party. At Ludhiana, Simpson visited the Fort (Fig. 17) which lay to the north-west of the city. At Kartarpur he drew the temple (Fig. 18), the schoolmaster (Fig. 19) and the son of the temple guru (Fig. 20). At Lahore another great Durbar was held where Lord Canning received three hundred Sikh sirdars, for this martial race had shown great loyalty during the troubles. Again it was a brilliant scene for an artist – the glorious colours of the costumes making it 'like a garden of flowers in motion', as Simpson noted. From here he went on to Peshawar, with its wonderful variety of races and types. On the way Simpson sketched a linseed-oil mill (Fig. 21), for agricultural implements and methods were another of his interests. In Peshawar itself a great torchlit procession was held to celebrate the arrival of Lord Canning in the Punjab (Fig. 22). Simpson even went on up to Jamrud, where he sketched the Khyber Pass (Fig. 23). Meanwhile the Governor-General's party had gone to Sialkot, where Ranbir Singh, the Maharaja of Kashmir (Fig. 24), was received at a great durbar (Fig. 25). Simpson was fascinated by the mixture of people among the Maharaja's followers – there was even an Afghan (Fig. 26). He was greatly amused by an incident at the durbar which indicated the lowly regard with which Indian artists were regarded by their countrymen. The Maharaja had brought his artist with him and asked the Governor-General's permission for the man to draw him. Permission being given, the artist crawled out from under a sofa opposite Lord Canning, where he had been hidden away. 'To see the man squeezing himself out was like a scene in a farce', Simpson noted.

The Governor-General's party now set off for Simla, as the hot weather had started on the Plains. Simpson, however, wishing to record further scenes and monuments, returned to Lahore, where he sketched the Moti Bazaar (Fig. 27), the Mausoleum of the Emperor Jahangir on the banks of the Ravi river (Figs. 28, 29), and the Char Burj (Fig. 30). He also drew the Mosque of Wazir Khan (Fig. 31) and the Elephant Gate to the Palace (Fig. 32), which had once been the private entrance to the apartments of the emperor and his ladies. Moving on to Amritsar, Simpson recorded the Golden Temple (Figs. 33, 34), where he also drew a priest reading the Holy Granth (Fig. 35). Increasingly, he was turning his attention and his pencil to the everyday lives of ordinary Indians. He was intrigued by the pony-carts called *ekkas* (Fig. 36) which crowded the streets, and, with his keen interest in handicrafts, was delighted to find that the city was full of workshops where, at every turn, he encountered craftsmen and women weaving and embroidering shawls and rugs (Figs. 37, 38). He toured the nearby countryside, too, and his fascination for simple technical ingenuity is reflected in his drawing of a Persian wheel raising water out in the fields (Figs. 39,40) – for the hot season had well and truly set in. It was time to move up into the hills.

Calcutta, from the maintop masthead of Green's ship "The Newcastle". Off Fort Point. 12ᵗʰ Nov. 1859.

D.432-1900.

1 Calcutta seen from the maintop of the *Newcastle*, 12 November 1859.

2 Government House, Calcutta, November 1859.

3 Native School, Calcutta, December 1859.

Barrackpore
17th Dec 1859

4 The garden of Barrackpore House near Calcutta, 17 December 1859.

Cashmere Gate Delhi
6ᵗʰ Jan. 1860

5 The Kashmir Gate, Delhi, 6 January 1860.

Mosque Piquet
Ridge before Delhi
8 January 1860

6 'Mosque Piquet, ridge before Delhi', 8 January 1860.

7 Mosque at the Custom House, Delhi, 9 January 1860.

8 The Lahore Gate of the Palace, Delhi, 9 January 1860.

9 The Burra Daribah, Delhi,
13 January 1860.

10 Chandni Chauk, Delhi,
13 January 1860.

23

11 Lal Kuan (the Red Well),
Delhi, 16 January 1860.

12 Humayun's Mausoleum, Delhi, 19 January 1860.

13 The canal at Roorkee, (January 1860) 1863.

14 The Raja of Patiala,
Ambala, 20 January 1860.

Rajah Patiallah

The Rajah of
Jheend
20th
Jan 1860

15 The Raja of Jhind,
Ambala, 20 January 1860.

Hindoo Temple at Sirhind
28th Jany. 1860

16 Hindu Temple, Sirhind, 28 January 1860.

17 Gate of the Fort, Ludhiana, 29 January 1860.

Kartarpore
2. Feb. 1860.

18 Temple, Kartarpur,
2 February 1860.

मित्रागसिंघ

Soodahgur Singh

Schoolmaster
Kartarpore 2 Feb 1860

19 The Schoolmaster,
Kartarpur, 2 February 1860.

ਸਾਹਿਬ ਦਾ ਜਵਾਹਿਰ ਸਿੰਘ ਜੀ

Sahib Jewahir Sing gee

Son of the goroo
Kartarpore 2nd Feb. 1860

20 Jawahir Singh, son
of the Guru, Kartarpur,
2 February 1860.

21 Linseed oil mill, Peshawar, 25 February 1860.

22 Illuminations at Peshawar, February 1860.

The Khyber Pass
From Jamrood 1st March 1860

23 The Khyber Pass, 1 March 1860.

Ranbir Singh
Maharajah of Cashmere
– 9th March 1868

24 Ranbir Singh, Maharaja of
Kashmir, 9 March 1860.

25 Durbar at Sialkot. Lord Canning with the Maharaja of Kashmir, 9 March 1860.

26 An Afghan, March 1860.

The Motee Bazaar Lahore
18th March 1861

27 Moti Bazaar, Lahore,
18 March 1860.

28 A minaret of Jahangir's mausoleum, Shahdara, near Lahore, 19 March 1860.

29 Cenotaph of Jahangir, Shahdara, (March 1860).

Chowbourjee
Lahore
21st March 1860
Charboorje

30 The Char Burj, Lahore,
21 March 1860.

31 Mosque of Wazir Khan, Lahore, (March 1860) 1864.

Hathi Durwaza
Elephant Gate
28 March 1860

Lohgurh Gate

32 The Elephant Gate of the Palace, Lahore, 28 March 1860.

33 Bathing steps of the Golden Temple, Amritsar, 30 March 1860.

34 The Golden Temple, Amritsar, (March 1860) 1864.

35 A Sikh reading the Granth, Amritsar, (March 1860) 1864.

36 Figure studies and *ekkas*, Amritsar, 30 March 1860.

37 Shawl workers sewing, Amritsar, 29 March 1860.

38 Shawl weavers, Amritsar, 31 March 1860.

Persian wheel
Amritsar 31st March 1860

39 Persian wheel, Amritsar, 31 March 1860.

40 Persian wheel, Amritsar, (March 1860) 1865.

The First Himalayan Tour

APRIL TO AUGUST 1860

Simpson made his way to Simla and rejoined the Governor-General's party. A watercolour (Fig. 41) probably shows Lady Canning making her way among the flowering rhododendrons for which these hills were famous. He seems quickly to have had his fill of the monotonous life of the Club, however, for he began to make excursions into the hills; he met and sketched the Rana of Bulsan (Fig. 42), and was delighted by the wooden temples (Fig. 43) and palaces (Fig. 44) of the Bashahr Raja. He became eager to explore deeper into the Himalayas. A number of adventurous East India Company servants such as Moorcroft, Hearsey, Trebeck, James Baillie Fraser and Gerard had earlier made expeditions into these Tibetan mountains, but there were as yet few visual records of the area apart from Fraser's *Journal of a Tour through Part of the Snowy Range of the Himala Mountains* of 1820. Simpson therefore jumped at the chance of joining an expedition led by a Captain Evans to Chini, some 10,000 feet high in the Sutlej valley, and sixteen marches from Simla.

They left Simla on 9 June and followed 'the Hindostan and Tibet Road, one of the works of Lord Dalhousie, who did things on a grand scale'. Simpson was awestruck by 'the Sutlej river some three thousand feet beneath, and the snowy peaks glittering some ten or twelve thousand feet overhead'. During the march, Simpson was delighted to see the villagers bringing their goats down to the lower ranges, the animals loaded with bags of pashmina wool tied on their backs, the main export of the area. He was also intrigued by the way the villagers smoked jointly,

lying like the spokes of a wheel around a hole in the ground where tobacco was burning, the smoke finding its way out through little tunnels. The landscape gradually changed from forest to bare rock, and Simpson had the hair-raising experience of crossing the foaming headwaters of the Sutlej by rope-bridge (Fig. 45). At Kanum he met and sketched a Lama (Fig. 46) and a nun in her red robe (Fig. 47); he visited a Buddhist temple and recorded some of the images it held (Fig. 48), and sketched weavers at their work (Fig. 49).

At Chini he drew a hill-woman (Fig. 50), meticulously noting details of her dress and jewellery. But perhaps the most memorable experience was the remarkable religious ceremony he witnessed at the village of Kothi (Fig. 51). The village men were carrying a wooden frame somewhat like a palanquin on their shoulders decorated 'by pieces of silk of various colours which hung down all round, and a piece of red cloth hung over the staves on each side, covering them except where they touched the men's shoulders. Above the level of the staves were fixed a number of masks of the Devi made of gold or brass. The central part of the structure was surmounted by a thick mass of yak's tails dyed red.' The party stopped and, still carrying the images, danced in front of the temple. Leading the procession were musicians playing drums and long S-shaped trumpets. The masks were washed in mint and water and kids were sacrificed, their heads offered to the Devi, drops of blood flicked on to the masks, the blood drained into a bowl and offered to the shrine. The meat was cooked and a feast held in the evening. Walnuts and pine cones were offered to the onlookers and thrown in a mock battle. The Kothi procession then moved on to visit the neighbouring village, whose Devi image met them at the entrance and eventually accompanied the visitors back to Kothi. (Simpson later wrote an article for the *Journal of the Royal Asiatic Society* describing the festival and speculating on its possible relationship to the procession of the ark in Egypt and the Jagannath car in Puri.)

On 28 August the party left Chini to begin the march back to Simla. Simpson sketched a temple at Chargaon (Fig. 52), knowing that the drawings he had made were among the very first to illustrate the life of this area.

41 Travelling by *jampan*, Simla, (April 1860) 1864.

42 The Rana of Bulsan,
4 May 1860.

Dan ka makan
or Hindoo Temple 25th May 1860
near Simla

43 Temple of the Devi near Simla, 25 May 1860.

44 Residence of the Raja of Bashahr at Serahn, 18 June 1860.

59

45 Rope Bridge over the Sutlej, near Chini, August 1860.

46 Sarup Jurgeon, Lama of
Leepee, 10 August 1860.

Hishiemull Sana woman
Kanum 11ᵗʰ August 1860

47 'Hishiemull', a nun at Kanum,
11 August 1860.

shekatoobah

Sherryboo
Meeyungadi ⎱ angels on each side
⎰ of shekatoobah

Idols of the Llamas of Kanum
12 August 1860

ཤཱཀྱ་ཐུབ་པ Shakya bdak-po

Lord Shakya (desire) founder of the
Buddhist Religion

48 Buddhist images, Kanum, 12 August 1860.

49 Weaver at Kanum, 12 August 1860.

50 Hiramal, a woman of Chini
and details of her jewellery,
18 August 1860.

51 Worship of the Devi at Kothi, near Chini, (August 1860).

52 Temple at Chargaon, 29 August 1860.

Down Country

The hot weather on the plains having now come to an end, Simpson left Simla on 9 October and returned to Delhi, where he sketched the Selimgarh Fort (Fig. 53), some intriguing doorways (Figs. 54, 55) and the famous Mutiny site of the Flagstaff Tower (Fig. 56), a building which the British had found valuable as an observation post after its capture on 20 September 1857.

Simpson had wanted to find out more about the lives of the women of India, and an opportunity to do so now came his way. He was staying in Delhi with a Mr Wagentreiber, editor of the *Delhi Punch*, who was married to an Anglo-Indian lady, a descendant of the famous Colonel Skinner of Skinner's Horse. One of their sons was married to a Kashmiri lady, so Mrs Wagentreiber arranged for Simpson to visit this lady, when she and her daughter would array themselves in their finery and jewellery and show him their home (Fig. 57). Simpson was delighted with the jewellery and intrigued by their dress, for, he wrote, 'a small silken vest, trimmed with a gilt edging, merely covers the breasts. Between the very small vest and the pyjamas there is a pretty large hiatus in the costume, which might rather astonish a European lady' (Fig. 58). He was also interested in the various household objects, such as the flat cushions, the betel-nut box, the spittoon and flower vases (Fig. 59). 'I have often seen "The Light of the Harem" in pictures', he noted, 'but in no instance have I ever seen anything that has the slightest resemblance to the truth of it.'

At the beginning of November Simpson moved on, stopping at Mathura (Fig. 60) and the deserted city of Fatehpur Sikri to draw the Buland Darwaza (Fig. 61), before reaching Agra. Exploring the Fort, he began to sketch the so-called Gates of Somnath (Fig. 63). It was generally believed that when Muhammad of Ghazni had sacked the temple of Somnath, he had carried off the great sandalwood gates as a trophy to be erected on his own tomb. At the end of the first Afghan War the British army had brought back the gates, which Lord Ellenborough replaced in the Fort in a splendidly propagandistic gesture 'as evidence to the people of India that our soldiers had been victorious in Afghanistan'. Simpson found his scepticism growing: 'Sketching leads one to notice details as well as to think.' He was convinced that the carving and ornament of the gates were Muslim, not Hindu, work. Simpson voiced his doubts to several 'men of position', including Lord Canning, all of whom assured him that 'there could be no doubt in the case, as every one referred to Lord Ellenborough's proclamation'. Clearly, the provenance of these old wooden doors was still – or again – a matter of political significance. Simpson would not let go so easily, however; back in England after his Indian tour, he discussed the matter with the famous archaeologist, James Fergusson, who agreed that the decoration was Muslim. Moreover, he had specimens of the wood examined at the British Museum and these proved to be of deodar pine rather than sandalwood. Simpson published an article on the gates and was delighted when the information was later included in Keane's *Guide to Agra*. He developed a keen and acute eye for Mughal architecture, sketching the Jami Masjid (Figs.

62, 64) and visiting the Taj Mahal. He was scathing about what he called 'Taj-worship' among vistors to India; the monument, though magnificent, he saw to be a comparatively late example of Mughal architecture and definitely inferior to many of the earlier monuments which were totally disregarded by the British. 'Very few people pay any real attention to the details of architecture', he notes.

At the end of his third week in Agra Simpson left for Cawnpore, where he sketched the famous 'Slaughter Ghat' (Fig. 65) and other places connected with the events of two years before. By the end of November he was in Lucknow (Fig. 66). 'The various localities in Lucknow connected with the memorable defence, as well as the siege operations for the relief of the defenders, required some time', he wrote; and over the next few days he toured these sites, producing a series of calm and curiously moving sketches which are among the most remarkable of the trip. The stark shell of the Residency (Fig. 67) is labelled in Simpson's sketch with forensic exactitude to show the room in which Havelock, after twelve pitched battles to enter the building, was killed. The nearby Bailey Guard Gate (Fig. 68) had been a key position in the defence of the Residency; the Mess House (Fig. 69) was where the European 32nd Regiment had held out. Simpson sketched Havelock's grave (Fig. 70) with its celebrated mango tree. The

British had suffered especially heavy losses at the Sikandra Bagh (Fig. 71). But Simpson was interested also in the elaborate architecture of the Nawab's palaces and public buildings with their elaborate stucco decoration, of which the Mermaid Gate of the Kaisarbagh (Fig. 72) was an outstanding example.

From Lucknow Simpson preceded, by way of Allahabad, to Benares, where he found much to interest him. He drew the great river with its famous ghats (see jacket front) and painted the Golden Temple (Fig. 73), where he was intrigued by the mantric chanting of a holy-man, which at the time seemed to Simpson a 'manifestation of mumbo-jumbo'. The artist later accosted him at the ghats with a friendly 'bum bum bo', which was his best approximation to the mantra, by way of striking up an acquaintance. Another new acquaintance was that of Raja Narain Singh, the Raja of Benares, who not only ordered his favourite dancing-girl to perform for Simpson but also provided his son (Fig. 74) as a subject, specially dressed for the occasion in his finest clothes. Simpson was also able to visit the famous Buddhist site of the stupa at Sarnath (Fig. 75), which is recorded in his watercolour as it was before the Archaeological Survey Department had been formed and restoration carried out. Stupas continued to hold a fascination for Simpson during subsequent tours.

Bridge of the Selimghur
16. Oct. 1860

53 The bridge, Selimgarh Fort, Delhi, 16 October 1860.

54 Doorway, Delhi,
22 October 1860.

Doorway in Delhi
22nd Oct 1860

55 A jeweller's shop, Delhi,
23 October 1860.

Flagstaff Tower Delhi
23 Oct 1860

56 Flagstaff Tower, Delhi, 23 October 1860.

Interior of a Zenana
at Delhi 24ᵗʰ Oct 1860

57 Interior of a *zenana*,
24 October 1860.

58 Shahzada Begum,
ornaments and auspicious red
hand mark, 25 October 1860.

4

Pandan

Changairdan
for flower

Gow Takea

vessels of the zenana
24th oct 1860

59 Furnishings
and vessels of
the *zenana*, 24
October 1860.

60 Mathura, (November 1860) 1865.

61 The Buland Darwaza, Fatehpur Sikri, (November 1860) 1862.

Juma Musjid
Agra 8. Nov 1860

62 The Jami Masjid, Agra, 8 November 1860.

The Gates of Somnath
agra 10 nov. 1860

See p. 125 in autobiography

63 The Gates of Somnath, Agra,
18 November 1860.

The Eastern end of the
Juma Musjid Agra
19 Nov 1860

64 Eastern end of the
Jami Masjid, Agra,
19 November 1860.

81

Hindoo Temple
at the Slaughter Ghat.
Cawnpore 23 Nov 1860.

65 'Slaughter Ghat',
Cawnpore,
23 November 1860.

66 General view of Lucknow, (November 1860) chromo-lithograph, 1865.

67 The Residency, Lucknow, 28 November 1860.

The Residency Lucknow
28th Nov 1860

85

68 The Bailey Guard Gate,
Lucknow,
29 November 1860.

The Bailey Guard Gate
Lucknow 29: Nov. 1860

The 32nd Mess House
Lucknow 30th Nov 1860

69 The 32nd Mess House, Lucknow, 30 November 1860.

70 Havelock's Grave, Alambagh, near Lucknow, 2 December 1860.

Secundra Bagh
Lucknow 4 Dec 1860

71 The Sikandra Bagh, Lucknow, 4 December 1860.

Mermaid Gate. Kaisar Bagh. Lucknow.   Wm Simpson 1864.

1136 '89

72 The Mermaid Gate,
Kaisarbagh, Lucknow,
(December 1860) 1864.

73 Nandi sculpture, Golden Temple, Benares, (December 1860) 1866.

Baboojah ChurMet Sing
Son of the Maharajah of Benares
Rammuggar 29ᵗʰ Dec 1860

74 Son of the
Maharaja of
Benares, 29
December 1860.

75 The Stupa, Sarnath,
    (January 1860) 1864.

93

Central India

JANUARY TO MARCH 1861

The new year brought a change of scene for Simpson. Lord and Lady Canning were about to make a cold-weather tour of Central India, visiting the various rajas and chiefs, especially Holkar of Indore and the Begum of Bhopal, who had remained loyal during the Mutiny. Durbars were to be held at these various courts. On this tour Simpson saw a very different landscape. The party set off in January following the old Deccan Road. They visited Mirzapur, a city on the Ganges noted for its handmade rugs and carpets. The city had a picturesque river-front with steep ghats (Fig. 76) and fine temples. Here the party visited one of the landlords, Tansuk Das (Fig. 77). They then went on to Jabalpur, where Simpson, with his interest in social change in India, was fascinated by the 'School of Industry' which had been set up to train former Thugs to adjust to society and learn the trade of carpet-weaving (Fig. 78). Simpson was particularly struck by a fine-looking ex-Thug (Fig. 79). He found it hard to believe that 'such a mild old man could have been an actor in the cold-blooded murders of the gang he belonged to. It was a curious sight', he wrote, 'to see these people, most of them boys and girls, the children of murderers. There were some old men who had no doubt used the *roomal*, the handkerchief with which the Thugs strangled their victims.' The Governor-General's party made an excursion to the famous Marble Rocks and temple (Fig. 80), a trip made partly by river and partly on elephants (Fig. 81).

After some twelve days at Jabalpur, camp was struck (Fig. 82) in preparation for a move east. Simpson, however, had decided that the time had come for a parting of the ways, as he now felt the wish to see more of Central India and Rajasthan in his own informal manner.

By now he had learned something of the language and he thoroughly enjoyed travelling rough in a light palanquin, sharing the food of the coolies who carried him. 'The ordinary traveller', he wrote, 'who "does" India, sees Bombay, Calcutta, Benares, Agra and Delhi, but the vast spaces between these noted places he sees nothing of.' He travelled with ten coolies, 'four to carry the *dhooly* and luggage, four to change with them, one *bhangy-wallah* who carried my luggage in a couple of baskets by means of a *bhangy* or piece of wood on his shoulder and a *masalchi* to carry the torch, for the men carried me at night, while I slept in the *dhooley*, which formed a sort of bed'. They rested during the day, which gave Simpson a chance to sketch. In this way he was able to see the real village life of India in places off the beaten track, which few Europeans ever saw. With a prescience which was certainly not shared by the company he had just left, Simpson wrote of these villages: 'They were there when we arrived in India, they were there when the Mohammedans came, and were probably on the same spot when Alexander crossed the Indus. To this it may be added that these villages will still be there when we leave India, whenever that may take place.' Among the sights he saw was the 'Bhilsa Tope', the famous Sanchi stupa (Fig. 83). He had difficulty in finding it, for he asked the coolies to take him to 'the tope', the word which he had heard used in north India to describe the Mankyala stupa. In Central India, however, the word 'tope' meant 'a cannon', and Simpson found himself being shown an old gun under a tree. When at last he tracked down the stupa, he found it, like all the others he had seen, in a ruined state, covered with vegetation. His careful sketch of this impressive structure is a valuable record of the state of the building before restoration. From here, Simpson now moved on to Bhopal (Fig. 84), some twenty miles to the east, and then, via Indore and Nimach, to Udaipur, capital of the Rajput state of Mewar. He was delighted with the superb setting of the Palace in a great artificial lake with two islands (Fig. 85). 'Since I have seen this town,' he wrote, 'I have always classed it, Malta and Edinburgh as the three finest cities that I have visited.' Simpson's interest in Hindu architecture was growing, and he realised that most of what he had seen up until now had been Muslim in style and inspiration. He visited the Temple of Jaganath (Fig. 86) – but, as always, did not overlook the interest of the humble and everyday (Fig. 87).

Time, however, was now getting short, so Simpson pressed on to Chitor, where he sketched the famous Tower of Victory (Fig. 88). He had been reading Colonel James Tod's *Annals of Rajasthan* as he travelled along, and now recalled the account of the great siege of Chitor by the Muslims, when the women and children all committed *johar* and were burnt to death while their menfolk met their death fighting the invaders. Simpson was deeply impressed by the sight of this deserted city: 'The walls and gates still remain. Within are towers, temples, and palaces, with here and there a village or two that has grown up among the silent streets.'

76 The ghats, Mirzapur, 7 January 1861.

77 Tansuk Das, a landlord,
Mirzapur, 7 January 1861.

78 The School of Industry, Jabalpur, 18 January 1861.

shoke Lall
a Thug Soindah (approver)
of the Nizams dominion.

naygeeb a Thyggee Policeman.

figures in to school of Industry
Jubblepore 18th Jan 1861

79 Ex-Thugs, School of Industry, Jabalpur, 18 January 1861.

80 Temple at the Marble Rocks, Jabalpur, 19 January 1861.

Shikāre Hathi
Juthulpore 23ʳᵈ Jan 1861

81 Elephant, Jabalpur, 23 January 1861.

82 Striking the Governor-General's camp, Jabalpur(?), January 1861.

83 The Sanchi Stupa, (February 1861) 1862.

84 View of Bhopal, (February 1861) 1864.

85 The Lake, Udaipur, Rajputana, 20 February 1861.

Temple of Juggernath. Oodeypoor. Rajpootana. 22nd Feb. 1861.

D.552-1900

86 Temple of Jaganath, Udaipur, 22 February 1861.

87 Old house, Udaipur, 23 February 1861.

88 Tower of Victory, Chitor,
26 February 1861.

The Second Himalayan Tour

APRIL TO OCTOBER 1861

By the end of March Simpson was back in Agra and the hot weather had begun. As he had been to Simla the previous year, he now decided to spend the hot weather exploring the hills from Mussoori. On 19 April he set off up the valley of the Ganges to its source at the Cow's Mouth. The trek was far more arduous than that of the prevous year. Simpson met up with two army officers and along with them, their servants and guides, he set off by the Hill road for the hot springs and snowy peaks of Jumnotri and Gangotri. Simpson sketched the small temple at Gangotri (Fig. 89), some twenty miles from the edge of the glacier from which the Ganges issues. This was reached the next day, Simpson noting that it was 'a very small stream of muddy stuff'. He nevertheless observed the Hindu rite of purification: 'I had my morning dip below the glacier, and I drank a little of the water.'

All had gone well on the way up but on the return journey it began to rain heavily, and then to snow. Simpson had some terrifying experiences when crossing the flooded river, scrambling over great rocks with water up to his chest. Then they had to cross the river again, balancing on pine-logs laid across the torrent. At the village of Kasauli there was an important temple and Simpson again saw a procession with a deity being carried along. While crossing the Manja Kanta pass at some 13,000 feet, the party suffered snow-blindness; then they made their way over the Roopin Pass, said to be as high as Mont Blanc. At Soonum Simpson was fascinated by the variety of praying machines (Fig. 90), some driven by water. He was also amazed to see children sleeping out of doors in spite of the intense cold (Fig. 91). The party had by now rejoined part of the route to Chini that Simpson had followed the previous year. They crossed the Parung and Tanglung Passes at 18,000 feet, where Simpson noted with curiosity the cairns with their prayer flags. Snow fell again and Simpson had his worst experience – he slipped down a crevasse. Luckily it was narrow and his arms caught on the sides so he was saved, but, he wrote, 'On kicking away more of the thin sides, I could see the dark cavern below. Icicles hanging down suggested teeth to my thoughts and it seemed like the mouth of a dreadful beast ready to swallow whatever came within reach.'

Finally, the party reached the Indus, where Simpson sketched the praying cylinders in the village of Kulsi (Fig. 92). There followed a long stretch through what was for Simpson 'bleak, uninteresting country', although he delighted in the Lama monasteries encountered on the way, and the courtesy and hospitality of the monks. At last they reached Sonamarg. 'I had then left the bleak country', Simpson records, 'and found myself in Kashmir, among luxuriant vegetation and beautiful flowers.' They arrived in Srinagar on 31 July, where they became the guests of the Government Agent, General van Cortlandt. He was most hospitable. His daughters were just back from school in Europe and the girls were anxious that Simpson should give them drawing-lessons. So Simpson went on many sketching tours, sometimes being rowed in the General's *shikara* over the lotus-studded lake (Fig. 93).

On one occasion they went to the Shalimar Garden, where the cascades at night were lit by candles in niches behind them. Nauch girls danced and sang *Taza-be-taza*. It was like a scene from *Lalah Rookh*! 'We seemed not to belong to the nineteenth century', Simpson wrote. 'The Peris of Paradise were not a matter of doubt; they were realities before us.' He described 'the sweet delusions of a never to be forgotten night. Had jinn or a giant appeared amongst us or – a Peri from Paradise, such an appearance would not have been thought out of place.' Simpson drew the extraordinary bridges and canals (Figs. 94, 95) of this 'mountain Venice', as he called it.

The General arranged a trip to Islamabad, and Simpson visited the nearby ruined temple of Martand (Fig. 96). Lord Canning had asked Simpson, if he happened to visit Kashmir, to collect the portraits of Ranbhir Sing and his son which had been promised to him while at the Sialkot Durbar. This he did. The party then visited Jammu State and Chamba. Simpson had originally hoped to extend his tour even further to Multan and Karachi, but a letter now reached him from Lord Canning requesting him to return to Allahabad by early November so that he could be present and paint a picture of the first Investiture of the Star of India, a new Order which Lord Canning had just inaugurated. The Order was to be a reward for those rulers who adopted modern ideas and social improvements. The first four princes honoured in this way were Scindia, Patiala, the Begum of Bhopal and the Nawab of Rampur. Allahabad had been chosen for the ceremony because of its central position. Canning had been so generous to Simpson that he could not but obey. He hastily returned and was present at the ceremony, though he was suffering from malaria at that time and his hand kept shaking as he drew. The contrast with his recent sense of freedom and well-being could not have been sharper. 'In all my experience', he wrote, 'I know of no more pleasant kind of existence in this world than that of wandering about in the Himalayas.'

89 Temple at Gangotri, 5 May 1861.

90 Praying cylinder in a Lama
monastery, (May-July 1861)
1862.

91 Children sleeping out of doors in the Himalayas, (May-July 1861) 1864.

Praying Cylinders in the village of Kulsi on the Indus.

92 Praying cylinders in the village of Kulsi, (July 1861) 1862.

93 'The Lake of Kashmir', 2 August 1861.

94 The Second Bridge, Srinagar, 11 August 1861.

The First Bridge, Srinugger, Cashmere, 13. Augt. 1861.

D.653-1900

95 The First Bridge, Srinagar, 13 August 1861.

96 The temple at
Martand, Kashmir,
August-September
1861.

South India and Bombay

NOVEMBER 1861 TO FEBRUARY 1862

Simpson's last tour took him to the South and to Bombay. He landed on 13 November through the surf at Madras on a masula boat (Fig. 97), a tiny craft made of planks of wood sewn together with coconut fibre. It was here that he heard the news of the death of Lady Canning from malignant malaria caught while touring in the mountains near Darjeeling. Simpson had hoped to travel to Bombay overland from Madras so that he could visit and draw a number of the famous South Indian temples on the way. He soon realised, however, that the time this would take made the journey impracticable, so it was arranged that he should go by sea on a Government steamer via Ceylon and call at various ports on the way. He caught a glimpse of Ceylon at Point de Galle and stopped at Quilon and Cochin on the Malabar Coast. The boat also called at Calicut, Cannanore and Mangalore. Simpson had a great wish to see the famous Gairsoppa Falls, the 'Niagara of the East', so he landed at Honawar and went ashore in a small dug-out boat, a terrifying experience as the rollers were immense. Setting out for the solitary trip to the Falls, Simpson writes, 'as I should be in the jungle, with nobody to see me, I left even my necktie behind'. But on arriving at his destination, he found the party of an official he had met in the Punjab. 'He insisted that I should be one of his party, but I pointed to my whole wardrobe, which consisted of the clothes I had on.' The loan of a tie, however, enabled him to join the company, who were in full evening-dress, for dinner. The sight of the Falls the next day impressed Simpson enormously. 'I can never forget', he wrote 'the grandeur of that roaring mass of water, the foam apparently falling from the sky above our heads to an immeasurable abyss beneath our feet . . . Descending from such a height, a large portion of the water becomes spray or fine mist, and when the sun shines the arc of a rainbow gleams amongst it.' Simpson made a drawing (Fig. 98), but decided that only Turner could have done justice to such a scene.

Simpson now returned to the coast, where he decided to make the 350-mile journey to Bombay by a *patamar*, a small open boat carrying a cargo of *pan* leaves. His berth was merely a mat laid on top of the cargo, but he had a good view of the coast and reached Bombay ten days later on 23 December. Here he met Dr Bhau Daji, the famous Maratha Brahmin scholar and archaeologist whose name the Museum in Bombay now bears. Through him Simpson was able to meet a number of cultured Parsees and Hindus, and to visit a school for Maratha Brahmin girls (Fig. 99). Determined to see more historic Hindu sites, Simpson again set off on his own. From Ahmednagar he visited the Ellora caves (Fig. 100), where he stretched some of the intriguing carvings (Fig. 101). An encounter with a Yogi made a deep impression on him. As they sat on a bench, Simpson was struck by the ascetic's indifference to the rats at their feet. 'Why don't you kill them?' he asked. 'Why should I kill them?' was the man's reply. 'We people kill them', Simpson explained; 'We people do not', the Yogi responded. 'I was beaten by this ascetic, who sat there calm and cool, clad in little more than the wood ashes of his fire', he writes. Next he visited the caves at Ajanta (Fig.

102), where he found Robert Gill making copies of the frescoes later displayed at the Crystal Palace. He also went to Karla, where he was greatly excited by the carvings (Fig. 103). It was here also that engineers were tunnelling through the Western Ghats to build the railway, sections of which, like that at the Bhor Ghat, were now in operation (Fig. 104).

Returning to Bombay, Simpson drew some of the British monuments, like the Wellesley Fountain near Church Gate sculpted by Chantry (Fig. 105). Although made to commemorate the visits of the Marquis in 1801 and 1804, the monument had only recently been erected. He also visited an Armenian family and sketched their colourful costume (Figs. 106, 107). During his last days in the city, Simpson explored its streets and thoroughfares, sketchbook, as ever, at the ready to record his impressions of everyday life (Figs. 108, 109, 110). On 12 January 1862 he boarded the P & O steamer *Jeddo* for England. What struck him most forcefully on landing in Southampton was the lack of colour in England: 'After the bright colours of India, it seemed to me that the people went about with the appearance of black beetles.'

The Beach at Madras with massoola Boats. 16 Nov. 1861.

D.654-1900.

97 Masula boats at Madras, 16 November 1861.

98 The Gairsoppa Falls,
10 December 1861.

99 Maratha Brahmin Girls' School, Bombay, (January 1862) 1865.

Sculptured Elephant and Pillar. Kylas, Cave of Ellora. W. Simpson. 1860.

1147.69

100 The Ellora Caves,
(January 1862) 1866.

124

101 The Boar Avatar
Sculpture at Ellora,
19 January 1862.

Vishnoo in the varáha or Boar Avátar from the cave called the Rávani Ki Khai or Rávans ditch Ellora 19 Jan. 1862

102 Robert Gill copying the Ajanta frescoes, January 1862.

103 Sculpture at Karla,
3 February 1862.

Sculpture
Karli 3 Feb. 1862

104 The railway at the Bhor Ghat, 4 February 1862.

Wellesley Monument
6 Feb. 1862

105 The Wellesley Fountain, Bombay, 6 February 1862.

Shreereen Bai

106 An Armenian child,
Bombay, 7 February 1862.

39

Manuk Bia
Bombay 7. Feb 1862

107 Manuk Bia, an
Armenian lady, Bombay,
7 February 1862.

131

108 A Bombay street, 8 February 1862.

109 A Bombay street scene, (8 February 1862) 1875.

Bombay
8 Feb. 1862.

110 A Bombay street,
8 February 1862.

'Disaster'

On his return to London Simpson took rooms in Lincoln's Inn Fields and set to work on the immense task of working up the sketches which filled his notebooks into finished watercolours which could be transferred to stone for the chromo-lithographic process by which they were to be reproduced in the projected *magnum opus*. Some were exhibited as they were finished, and the response encouraged Simpson in his hopes for a major artistic and publishing event which would establish his reputation and place him on a secure financial footing – for he had used up all hs money to pay for the Indian trip.

Unknown to Simpson, however, his publishers, Day and Son, had been drifting badly into debt. In 1866, shortly after Simpson had delivered the last of the 250 watercolours, William Day decided as a last recourse to convert the business into a limited company. Day and Son Limited now owed the artist some £6000 in respect of the value of the work it held; William Day offered to make Simpson a shareholder in the new company as part payment. For some months there was no communication between the two men and Simpson went to Scotland, where news finally reached him that Day had put the company into the hands of the liquidator and had left the Board. Too late, it turned out that the 250 watercolours had been sold off as bankrupt stock. 'I had not a penny', Simpson wrote. 'Here was the reward of my seven years' work . . . This was the big disaster of my life.'

Some fifty of the illustrations had already been converted into lithographs, and the liquidators suggested that these should be published. Sir John Kaye, Secretary to the Secret and Political Department at the India Office, was persuaded to write an accompanying text. Simpson himself oversaw its production, although he was bitterly disappointed by the poor quality of the reproductions (see Fig. 66). The book came out in 1867 as *India Ancient and Modern*. It was well enough received, but Simpson was, for the time being, inconsolable. 'So the great work on India', he wrote, 'on which I had bestowed so much time and labour, never came into existence, and I lost the honour and reputation which would have been due to me if such a work had been properly produced and published.'

Yet, despite all this, the book was a success of sorts. Though the fashion for chromo-lithography had passed, supplanted by the steel engraving – a fact which was certainly partly to blame for Day's failure – the freshness and originality of Simpson's vision was widely appreciated. During the late eighteenth and early nineteenth centuries the British view had been largely based on the aquatints of William Hodges published in his *Select Views* (1786-88) and on Thomas and William Daniells' *Oriental Scenery* (1795-1808). Hodges had depicted for the first time many places in Upper India, especially the monuments in the Ganges Valley. The Daniells had pressed on further to Garhwal in the Himalayas. In the South they had explored the great hills of Mysore and Tinnevelly and had reached Cape Comorin. Just as Richard Wilson had introduced Italy to the British public through his oil paintings, so Hodges and the Daniells had begun to acclimatise India. Both artists had also introduced the British public to Indian architecture in the form of picturesque antiquities. They themselves had been educated within the accepted tradition of the classical ideal landscape and the picturesque. But to the Victorians this approach now seemed outdated. As Edward Lear commented when looking at one of Thomas Daniell's views of Benares after his own return from India: 'How well I remember the views of Benares by Daniell; pallid, gray, and solemn. I had always supposed this place a melancholy, or at least a staid and soberly-coloured spot, a record of bygone days. Instead I find it one of the most startlingly radiant places full of bustle and movement. Constantinople or Naples are simply dull and quiet by comparison.'

In the years before the appearance of *India Ancient and Modern*, many books of memoirs had been published by British amateur artists resident in India who were frequently skilled watercolourists. These accounts were often illustrated with lithographs after the author's own drawings depicting village scenes, the occupations of the people and picturesque monuments. These works, however, did not have a wide circulation and were usually acquired by people with Indian links who had either themselves worked in India or had relatives there. Simpson aimed at a much broader audience; he approached India in a completely new manner which he hoped would appeal to the general public.

Although Simpson had originally been sent to India to record the setting of the Mutiny events, his drawings did far more: they gave a far wider and more realistic picture of India. As Sir John Kaye enthusiastically noted in his foreword to *India Ancient and Modern* : 'There is scarcely an aspect of natural scenery, scarcely a work of art ancient or modern – scarcely a phase of human life, Native or European – that the artist has not endeavoured to render familiar to his home-staying countrymen.' The book and its plates proved highly popular and today is avidly collected. A number of the drawings which were sold off eventually reached the national collections, where they take their place as highly professional examples of Victorian painting. They are notable for their free use of watercolour washes and their great animation. Simpson had superb skill in catching the likeness of a person or a scene with a rapid sketch and it is the sketchbooks in particular with their lively line which perhaps best reflect his warm and excited response to the Indian scene. They gave a new picture of India – that newly acquired Jewel in the Crown.

BIBLIOGRAPHY

BOOKS BY WILLIAM SIMPSON

The Seat of the War in the East (1855)

India Ancient and Modern (1867) Text by Sir John Kaye

A Souvenir of the War of 1870-1 (1871)

The Abyssinian Expedition (1872)

Meeting the Sun: A Journey all round the World through Egypt, China, Japan and California (1874)

Picturesque People, being groups from all quarters of the globe (1876)

Shikare and Tomasha: A Souvenir of the Visit of HRH the Prince of Wales to India (1876)

The Autobiography of William Simpson RI (1903) Eyre-Todd ed.

ARTICLES BY WILLIAM SIMPSON

'Costume and jewellery worn by ladies of the Delhi zenana', *The Watchmaker, Jeweller and Silversmith*, October 1886

'Pujahs in the Sutlej Valley', *Journal of the Royal Asiatic Society*, 1884, vol. xvi, part I, pp. 13-30

'The Buddhist praying wheel, a collection of material bearing upon the symbols of the wheel and circular movements in custom and religious ritual', 1886

'The threefold division of temples', *Transactions of the Lodge Quatuor Coronati*, 1888, I, 89, no. 2076

'Classical influence in the Architecture of the Indus region and Afghanistan', *R I B A Journal*, 1894, I, 93, 147, 191

'The Bamian statues and caves', *R I B A Journal*, 1894, I, 527

'Abyssinian church architecture', *Architectural Review*, 1898, III, 245, IV, 9, 54

CREDITS